The Best Brothers

Also by Daniel MacIvor:

Never Swim Alone & This Is a Play
See Bob Run & Wild Abandon
The Soldier Dreams
I Still Love You
Marion Bridge
Arigato, Tokyo
His Greatness
How It Works
You Are Here
Cul-de-sac
One Voice
In On It
Monster
Bingo!

The Best Brothers
Daniel MacIvor

Playwrights Canada Press
Toronto

PLAYWRIGHTS CANADA PRESS
202-269 Richmond St. W., Toronto, ON M5V 1X1
416.703.0013 • info@playwrightscanada.com • www.playwrightscanada.com

We acknowledge the financial support of the Canada Council for the Arts,
the Ontario Arts Council, the Ontario Media Development Corporation,
and the Government of Canada through the Canada Book Fund for our
publishing activities.

 Canada Council **Conseil des Arts** **ONTARIO ARTS COUNCIL**
for the Arts **du Canada** **CONSEIL DES ARTS DE L'ONTARIO**

Cover photo of Buddy by Guntar Kravis
Book design by Blake Sproule

LIBRARY AND ARCHIVES CANADA CATALOGUING IN PUBLICATION
MacIvor, Daniel, 1962-
        The best brothers / Daniel MacIvor.

A play.
Issued also in electronic formats.
ISBN 978-1-77091-154-3

        I. Title.

PS8575.I86B48 2013   C812'.54   C2012-907930-8

First edition: April 2013
Printed and bound in Canada by Imprimerie Gauvin, Gatineau

To H.B. and Lucy

The Best Brothers received its world premiere on June 26, 2012, at the Stratford Shakespeare Festival Studio Theatre in Stratford, Ontario. The play featured the following cast and creative company:

Kyle Best: John Beale
Hamilton Best: Daniel MacIvor

Director: Dean Gabourie
Set designer: Julie Fox
Costume designer: Jessica Poirier-Chang
Lighting designer: Itai Erdal
Composer: Jonathan Monro
Sound designer: Jesse Ash
Dramaturge: Iris Turcott
Stage manager: Marylu Moyer

Characters

Hamilton Best
Kyle Best

Prologue: An Empty Field/A Penthouse

Light to two separate areas:

HAMILTON is holding rolled blueprints. He is in an empty field.

KYLE is holding a clipboard with a real-estate listing. He is in a penthouse.

They both speak to unseen clients, off.

HAMILTON: An empty space.

KYLE: A blank canvas.

HAMILTON: In the middle of nowhere.

KYLE: At the top of the world.

HAMILTON: Anything is possible.

KYLE: It's all up to you.

HAMILTON: The plans say a window here.

KYLE: This is your view.

HAMILTON: Imagine that a moment.

KYLE: Take it in.

HAMILTON: Take it in.

KYLE: A view like this?

HAMILTON: You can't pay for a view like this.

KYLE: It's priceless.

HAMILTON: I want you to have the space that you need.

KYLE: I need you to have the space that you want.

HAMILTON: Now I'm not a numbers person.

KYLE: So four twenty-five plus condo fees, three-and-a-half plus insurance, ballpark eighty-five or ninety per.

HAMILTON: I'm not trying to sell you anything.

KYLE: Approved at four point two five with fifty down you're carrying at twelve hundred.

HAMILTON: Take some time.

KYLE: Considering it just came on the market—

HAMILTON: It's one of the most important things you will ever do.

KYLE: It's now or never.

> KYLE *and* HAMILTON's *phones both ring.*

> *Both look at their call display.*

This looks like something, I better take it.

HAMILTON: Excuse me a moment.

They answer their phones.

HAMILTON & KYLE: *(on phones)* Hello?
Uh huh.
An accident?
Oh dear.
How is she?
I see.

KYLE: *(on phone)* So no rush then?

HAMILTON: *(on phone)* Yes yes of course, I'll be there right away.

KYLE: *(on phone)* Thanks.

They hang up their phones.

(to clients) Bit of a something something, nothing to be... just a something. Strange sort of... One of those things.

HAMILTON: Oh God.

KYLE: *(to clients)* I should probably...

HAMILTON: *(to clients)* There's been a terrible tragedy.

KYLE: *(to clients)* ...dash actually.
So, do you want to make an offer?

Blackout. Music.

The Obituary

KYLE's condo.

KYLE is sitting with a notepad, pencil and a newspaper section.

HAMILTON stands nearby.

KYLE: "Peacefully"?

HAMILTON: Peacefully?

KYLE: *(liking the sound of it)* Peacefully.

HAMILTON: "Peacefully"?

KYLE: *(writing it down)* "Peace-fully."

HAMILTON: You're not serious?

KYLE: It's very common.

HAMILTON: Where?

KYLE: *(indicating newspaper)* Here.
A series of templates.

HAMILTON: Templates?

KYLE: Examples.

HAMILTON: I know what a template is.

KYLE: *(indicating each)* "Peacefully." "Peacefully." "Peacefully." "Peacefully."

HAMILTON: Put that away.

KYLE: It'll be helpful.

HAMILTON snatches the paper from him.

HAMILTON: Put it away.

KYLE: Not peacefully?

HAMILTON: Really?

KYLE: How could we know?

HAMILTON: "Horribly" more like. "Dreadfully." "Hideously." "Atrociously." "Unspeakably."

KYLE: Well, not unspeakably.

HAMILTON: Not unspeakably?

KYLE: If it were unspeakable we shouldn't say anything.

HAMILTON: *(calmly)* I could kill you.

KYLE: Sorry.
It's hard to know where to start.

HAMILTON looks at the newspaper.

HAMILTON: "We are saddened."

KYLE: *(sighs)* Yes.

HAMILTON: Start there.

KYLE: Where?

HAMILTON: "We are saddened"!

KYLE: *(happily)* Ah yes, excellent!
(writing) "We… are… saddened…"
(He stops and thinks.) Um. "To…" "to…"? Not "report." Um.
To…?
(indicating newspaper) If I could just take a peek at—

HAMILTON: "Announce."

KYLE: Very good.
(writing) "We are saddened to announce the…"
Um…
Well not "peaceful."

HAMILTON: "Sudden."

KYLE: "Sudden"! "Sudden." Yes good "sudden." Sudden. Yes.
(suddenly sad) Sudden. Yes.

HAMILTON: Go on.

KYLE: "We are saddened to announce the sudden…"
Um.

> HAMILTON *glares at him.*

(proudly) "Passing of"!
That's good. "Passing of." Yes. That's better than the other. Softer.
Than, you know, *(darkly)* "death."

HAMILTON: Go. On.

KYLE: "We are saddened to announce the sudden passing of our
beloved…"
"…of our loving."
Our beloved? Our loving? Beloved or loving. Beloved would be
of us to her. Loving would be from her to us. Or anyone, not just
us. All people. All creatures. "Loving" would be more… Although
"beloved" would be more—

HAMILTON: *(calmly)* Just her name will do.

KYLE: Just her name will do. Of course you're right. That's easier. "We
are saddened to announce the sudden passing of Bunny Best."

HAMILTON: You can't call her "Bunny."

KYLE: Everyone called her Bunny.

HAMILTON: Not officially, not in the paper.

KYLE: Does it need to be official?

HAMILTON: It's an *obituary*, you can't get more official than that!

KYLE: Sorry.

HAMILTON: "Ardith."

KYLE: Some people won't know it's her.

HAMILTON: There'll be a picture.

KYLE: Really? What sort of picture?

HAMILTON: A picture that looks like her.

KYLE: So, a recent picture?

HAMILTON: If you want people to know that it's her.

KYLE: She wouldn't like that, she'd want something younger.

HAMILTON: Then how will people know that it's her?

KYLE: That's my point.

HAMILTON: Ardith "Bunny" Best. How's that?

KYLE: Oh that's good.
  (writing) "We are saddened to announce the sudden passing of
  Ardith "Bunny" Best surrounded by—"

HAMILTON: "Surrounded by"?

KYLE: Most of them say "surrounded by."

HAMILTON: Surrounded by who? Surrounded by what? Clowns and
  marching bands?

KYLE: I know but...

HAMILTON: But what?!

KYLE: If we can't say "surrounded by" can we say "peaceful"?

HAMILTON: Peaceful?! Peaceful?! How can we be back to peaceful?! What in God's name was peaceful about it?

KYLE: She's peaceful now.

HAMILTON: No she is not! She's hovering over us right now watching this ridiculous exercise! Writhing in horror at your stupidity!

KYLE: That's uncalled for.

HAMILTON: No it most certainly is not you moron! She met a tragic, disgusting, horrific end! There was nothing at all peaceful about it! There is nothing peaceful about manslaughter!

KYLE: It wasn't manslaughter Hamilton.

HAMILTON: Involuntary!

KYLE: It was an unfortunate accident.

HAMILTON: Fine Kyle fine, it was an accident. It was an accident that Mother was standing in the exact spot she was standing in at the Gay Days Parade when the Orthopaedic Hospital Gay Doctors Float came round the corner on Parliament Street. It was an accident that the fat Filipino drag queen had had too much cheap rum and lost her balance while she was lip-synching on a speaker to some inane disco anthem. It was an accident that as she fell she grabbed the speaker with her fat little fingers and the four-hundred-pound accumulated weight of speaker and drag queen *flattened* a one-hundred-and-two-pound seventy-five-year-old woman! That was the accident that killed our mother?

KYLE: Yes.

HAMILTON: So someone is responsible!

KYLE: I guess.

HAMILTON: Who?

KYLE: Mother?

HAMILTON: NO!

KYLE: She could have stayed home.

HAMILTON: But she didn't!
   (a beat; then quietly) And whose fault is that?

   A moment.

KYLE: "And whose fault is that"?

   HAMILTON says nothing.

   "And whose fault is that"?

HAMILTON: I'm sorry.

KYLE: Do you have something you'd like to say?

HAMILTON: No.
   I'm sorry.

KYLE: Here.
   (hands HAMILTON the notepad and pencil) You finish.

HAMILTON: *(taking the notepad and pencil)* Yes of course I'll finish. *(reviewing)* "We are saddened to announce blah blah blah Ardith "Bunny" Best."
(writing) "She is survived by her son... her loving son Kyle, and—"

KYLE: Thank you.

HAMILTON: You're welcome.

KYLE: Would it be wrong to put my business website there?

HAMILTON: Yes.

KYLE: Yes.

HAMILTON: *(writing)* "She is survived by her loving sons Kyle and Hamilton—"

KYLE: Parentheses Jules.

HAMILTON: Parentheses Jules?

KYLE: Parentheses Jules.

HAMILTON: Parentheses Jules what?

KYLE: Jules your wife.

HAMILTON: I know Jules is my wife.

KYLE: "Hamilton parentheses Jules." They all do that. "William parentheses Kate." "Mickey parentheses Minnie." "Bob parentheses Kevin." They all do that.

HAMILTON: *(writing)* "Hamilton parentheses Jules."
"Ardith was predeceased by her" no adjective necessary "former husband—"

KYLE: No adjective necessary.

HAMILTON: "Chuck Best."

KYLE: Not "Charles"?

HAMILTON: *(enjoying this)* Chuck.

KYLE: *(enjoying it as well)* Chuck.

HAMILTON: "Visitation will be held at—"

KYLE: Parentheses Candy.

HAMILTON: What?

KYLE: Chuck parentheses Candy.

HAMILTON: Chuck parentheses Candy.
I could kill you.

KYLE: I was just thinking out loud.

HAMILTON: That's not thinking. How is that thinking? You would think to mention the boneless bimbette that our father left our mother for in our mother's obituary?

KYLE: No.

HAMILTON: No?

KYLE: Yes.

HAMILTON: Then stop thinking.

KYLE: But that first Thanksgiving you liked Candy when she—

HAMILTON: Kill you.

KYLE: Geeze.

    A moment. HAMILTON *surveys his surroundings.*

HAMILTON: Have I been here before?

KYLE: Where?

HAMILTON: This apartment.

KYLE: No. I've only been here two months though.

HAMILTON: Where were you two months ago?

KYLE: Just off Church. But you weren't there either.

HAMILTON: Oh.

KYLE: I was only there for the winter.

HAMILTON: You might consider settling down at some point.

KYLE: Gordon was talking about getting a place together.

HAMILTON: Who?

KYLE: Gordon?

HAMILTON: Ugh. *(continues writing)* "Visitation will be held at blah blah blah and funeral service blah blah—"

KYLE: Um?

HAMILTON: Yes?

KYLE: I was just...

HAMILTON: Thinking?

KYLE: Ish.

HAMILTON: What?

KYLE: In terms of "survived by" we might like to mention...

HAMILTON: Who?

KYLE: Well...

HAMILTON: Jorge?

KYLE: Ah, she loved Jorge. He was so hairy. Guys were hairier then. He was a hippie though, hippies were all hairy.

HAMILTON: We're not mentioning Jorge.

KYLE: I wasn't thinking Jorge.

HAMILTON: Who? Marius?

KYLE: Oh Marius!

HAMILTON: Marius was an idiot.

KYLE: Marius took us to Alaska.

HAMILTON: Twelve-year-old boys do not want to spend summer vacation in Alaska.

KYLE: The whale-watching was beautiful.

HAMILTON: You cried the whole time.

KYLE: The whales were beautiful.
I liked Marius.

HAMILTON: Then you mention Marius in your obituary.

KYLE: I wasn't thinking Marius.

HAMILTON: Andre?!

KYLE: We could mention Andre.

HAMILTON: He slept with Deirdre!

KYLE: Oh, should we mention Deirdre?

HAMILTON: NO!

KYLE: No.
Anyway, I wasn't thinking Andre.

HAMILTON: Who then?

KYLE: Um…

HAMILTON: Who?

A beat.

KYLE: Enzo?

A beat.

HAMILTON continues making notes.

HAMILTON: I could kill you.

KYLE: But Mother would—

HAMILTON: Right now.

KYLE: But—

HAMILTON: With my mind.

KYLE: Okay. Geeze.

A beat.

How's he settling in?

HAMILTON: He's fine.

KYLE: Do he and Jules get along now?

HAMILTON: They avoid one another.

KYLE: That's probably good.

HAMILTON: Yes.

KYLE: I guess he's pretty broken up.

HAMILTON: He's not sleeping at all. I gave him some Valium.

KYLE: That's probably good.

HAMILTON: Yes.
> (*going over his notes*) Something about Pappa and Boo and Branksome Hall and her charity work and blah blah blah—I'll put that together later and finish up with, "In lieu of flowers—"

KYLE: Oh oh! Wait wait! "In lieu of flowers plant something pretty or feed a critter."

> *HAMILTON gives KYLE a look.*

I saw that in one of the templates. I thought we could borrow it.

HAMILTON: Perfect.

KYLE: Really?

HAMILTON: No.
> "In lieu of flowers donate to a charity of your choice."

KYLE: That's not very personal.

HAMILTON: They get to choose the charity, how much more personal could that be?

KYLE: That's true.

HAMILTON: *(writing)* "—donate to a charity of your choice." Period. There. Done. Right?

KYLE: Right.

HAMILTON: You're good with that?

KYLE: Yes.

HAMILTON: No more thoughts?

KYLE: No.

HAMILTON: Suggestions?

KYLE: No.

HAMILTON: Omissions?

KYLE: No.

HAMILTON: Good.

KYLE: Are you sure we shouldn't mention Enzo?

HAMILTON hits KYLE.

Ow!

Blackout.

Music. Light.

A hat box is produced and inside are a lady's hat and gloves.
KYLE holds the box and HAMILTON puts on the hat and gloves.
HAMILTON gently cradles KYLE's cheek in the palm of his gloved
hand. KYLE departs. With a flourish HAMILTON removes the hat,
holding it in his hand. With this gesture he assumes the char-
acter of his mother, Bunny. As Bunny, HAMILTON speaks to the
audience.

HAMILTON AS BUNNY: Planets and moons.
Protons and neutrons.
The nucleus sun.
How can we not see that?
Because we don't want to think of ourselves so tiny, or so large?

That thought came to me suddenly one strange July night. One of
many thoughts that came to me that strange night. But the main
thought made me a person I never thought I was.

And who was I? Ardith. Bunny. Mrs. Best. The former Mrs. Best.
A friend. A lover. A mother. Perhaps. But all of these conditional
on how I saw myself from the outside. Always viewing my orbit.
A planet in many universes but a sun in none. Never feeling…
enough. Which is what led my to my sudden strange July night
and the ceremony.

I am not at liberty to divulge the names of those involved in the ceremony since the "medicine"—that is what it is called by those who
ingest and administer it: "medicine"—is a Peruvian root known
for its psychotropic effects and very not legal at all.

Upon meeting my ceremony comrades—two intellectuals, an
incongruous blond, three hippies (hippies are still hairy, like
they always were) and a woodsy gentleman about my age who
would have been very interesting to me had I been interested

in gentlemen about my age—we together trekked deep into the woods, encountering blackflies the size of raven nestlings and what were said to be—by the woodsy gentleman—bear droppings.

Once in the shack we were each ensconced in a corner with our sleeping bags and purging buckets. Yes purging buckets. We set about taking the medicine and travelling... elsewhere... for several strange hours. For me it was... It was... Not what I expected. What did I expect? Warmth? Light? Bright space? Confirmation? Well there was a confirmation, but not an intellectual confirmation. It was... For me it was...? "Chilling" is a word. "Bleak" is a word. "Trudge" is a word. Trudge as defined by Webster is "to walk with purpose." The feeling had a trudginess about it. But the purpose... Ah the purpose.
Something cellular?
Inevitable?
Physics?
Very very small... and huge like a galaxy.
Sentimental yet nihilistic.
...?

Clearly I struggle to define this experience. Imagine... a Hallmark greeting card written by Nietzsche and illustrated by Einstein?

The next morning after the medicine had worn off we all had coffee—or for the hippies, dirt tea. The sun had risen and there was a sharing circle.

The hippies all spoke of the tunnels of the Knights Templar and spirit guides, the intellectuals mumbled, the incongruous blond cried, the woodsy gentleman told jokes and I, when it came round the circle to me, when I was to speak, I said, unplanned, unexpected, suddenly, I spoke these words:
"I am going to get a dog."

Light shift.

Music.

The Visitation (Part 1)

KYLE's condo.

HAMILTON sits.

KYLE stands nearby with a pencil and a calendar.

KYLE: We could do seven to nine Thursday and Friday evening, or two to five and seven to nine just on Friday.

HAMILTON: Whatever.

KYLE: The thing with one full day is more focus, the thing with the two evenings is more choice.

HAMILTON: It doesn't matter to me.

KYLE: Although if someone's bad in the evenings they're bad in the evenings. So in fact mixing it up with an afternoon and an evening is probably where you get the most choice.

HAMILTON: I guess.

KYLE: But two full days is just too much.

HAMILTON: Probably.

KYLE: So Thursday/Friday or Friday/Friday?

HAMILTON: Whatever.

KYLE: We kind of have to decide now-ish.

HAMILTON: It's up to you.

KYLE: It's up to me?

HAMILTON: Yes.

KYLE: Oh.
Okay.
Well then.

> KYLE *considers his options. He takes out some lip balm and puts it on.*

Hmmm.
Hmmmmmmmm.
Hmmmmmmmmmmmmmmmm.

> HAMILTON *struggles with growing annoyance.*

How about this…

> HAMILTON *looks to* KYLE.

No that's crazy. Wait…
Ummm.
Ummmmmmmm.
Ummmmmmmmmmmmmmmm.

HAMILTON: Jesus Kyle!

KYLE: It's hard.

HAMILTON: Just decide!

KYLE: Can we have fancy sandwiches?

HAMILTON: What?

KYLE: Can we have fancy sandwiches?

HAMILTON: At the visitation?

KYLE: Yeah.

HAMILTON: It's not an event to be catered.

KYLE: Any event is an event to be catered.

HAMILTON: We're not catering our mother's visitation.

KYLE: Actually catering might seem a little cold.
Or I could do it. I could make fancy sandwiches.

HAMILTON: No.

KYLE: It's easy. You take three layers of white bread and you use food colouring to colour the bread, say green and yellow and pink, or yellow and pink and orange, or green and yellow and orange, not blue, I saw blue fancy sandwiches once and they didn't seem fancy they seemed weird, and then you roll out the bread and make it flat and then you spread a layer of tuna and then a layer of—

HAMILTON: Tuna.

KYLE: Yeah.

HAMILTON: Tuna?

KYLE: Yeah.

HAMILTON: We're not serving tuna sandwiches at our mother's visitation.

KYLE: No, not just tuna, it has gherkins and olives and onions and—

HAMILTON: No.

KYLE: —sun-dried tomatoes and artichokes and sea salt—

HAMILTON: NO!

   Silence.

KYLE: We could get Jules to make the sandwiches.

HAMILTON: Jules is a chef.

KYLE: Exactly.

HAMILTON: She doesn't make sandwiches.

KYLE: We could call them "paninis."

HAMILTON: No.

KYLE: Maybe I could ask Gordon.

HAMILTON: Who?

KYLE: Gordon.

HAMILTON: Ugh.

KYLE: Maybe he could do something Jamaican.

HAMILTON: What? Like a pinata?

KYLE: A pinata is Mexican not Jamaican.

HAMILTON: A conga line?

KYLE: That's Cuban. And I'm talking about food. Maybe something jerk in a sandwich?

HAMILTON: We. Are not. Serving. Sandwiches.

Silence.

KYLE: What if we had a little thing after?

HAMILTON: A little thing?

KYLE: After. At the downtown condo maybe?

HAMILTON: Why are you determined to turn this into a soiree?!

KYLE: I'm not.

A beat.

Maybe not the condo though. I was thinking we should be staging the condo so it can be listed right away.

HAMILTON: List the condo?

KYLE: That's how it's done.

HAMILTON: So quickly?

KYLE: It's prime market.

HAMILTON: But…

KYLE: You want the condo?

HAMILTON: No but…

KYLE: What about the house?

HAMILTON: We're not selling the house!

KYLE: No I meant a little thing after at the house.

HAMILTON: Kyle…
    I don't think I can handle all that.

    A moment.

KYLE: How about Thursday evening seven to nine, then Friday two to
    five and seven to nine? Two evenings and an afternoon?

HAMILTON: That sounds fine.

KYLE: Good.

    A moment.

Can we serve chocolate cake?

HAMILTON: No!

KYLE: Come on!

HAMILTON: Chocolate cake?

KYLE: Chocolate cake! Remember?
Mother's tucking-in prayer.

HAMILTON: Mother hardly tucked us in.

KYLE: But when she did.
"Now I lay me down to sleep,
I beg the sheep my toes to keep,
I'll dream and dream and when I wake..." Remember?
Come on!

HAMILTON: No.
Kyle.
Please.

KYLE: Okay.
I'll call the funeral home.
Thursday/Friday/Friday?

HAMILTON: Fine.

KYLE: Okay.

KYLE *departs.* HAMILTON *is alone.*

HAMILTON: "I'll dream and dream and when I wake,
We'll celebrate with chocolate cake."

Light shift.

Music.

The hat box is produced.

HAMILTON *holds the box while* KYLE *puts on the hat and gloves.*

Gently KYLE *cradles* HAMILTON's *cheek in the palm of his gloved hand.*

HAMILTON *departs.*

KYLE *removes the hat and assumes the character of Bunny.*

KYLE AS BUNNY: I was never lonely. I considered that state an indulgence of the chronically lazy or the terminally privileged. "Oh there's nothing to do and no one to do it with." That was never me.

And then I met Charles. There was a time when I would have phrased that statement as, "And then I fell in love." But now I know better. I hear that all the time from women. The story of their early life, filled with promise and wonder and possibilities and then the line that turns the worm: "And then I fell in love." In a tone as if saying, "And then I lost the use of my legs." "And then I was diagnosed with malaria." "And then I stopped breathing."

So that was Charles. And then came Hamilton and then came Kyle. My sons. My boys. Whom I loved… differently, as different as they were. Hamilton moved like a warm tide. Kyle spurted like a fountain. Hamilton spoke. Kyle talked. Hamilton was good

with rooms full of people and how to get along. But Kyle was…
he was… a little… inside… outside… inside out. *(a moment)* The
real truth be told I did perhaps love Kyle a little… not more but…
harder. Because he needed it.

And then time speeds up in that annoying relativity it has and
Charles meets a small pink girl—showing himself to be far more
a Chuck than a Charles—and he leaves. Which is initially a relief.

Then the boys develop an unexpected affection for boarding
school. Which is initially exhilarating. But soon enough pattern
and routine reveal their hollowness and space spreads out that
needs to be filled.

So then there is a gaggle of formerly concessioned women like
myself—Maxine with her portable party and Hermes Helene and
Devious Deirdre—with whom I spent my time in airports and for-
eign hotels and my money on spas and shoes. But all that, that's
just spending.

And then there were the men: Van the mountain climber; and
Jorge, dear Jorge; and Marius and his regretful Alaskan adventure;
and Tony who loved Halloween and made the boys the best zombie
costumes anyone at Underwood Prep had ever seen; and Harald
the inevitable German and lastly the despicable Andre. Who didn't
do much of anything, other than to educate a series of women as
to the benefit of diligence over enthusiasm where vaginal orgasm
was concerned. But all that, that's just men.

And I saw, for the first time, I was lonely.
We are lonely.
We are all so lonely.
But don't lose hope.

Because perhaps for you too there will be a strange summer night as there was for me.

Light shift.

Music.

The Visitation (Part 2)

A *funeral home.*

A *podium and a visitor's book.*

The brothers greet a line of unseen passing mourners.

HAMILTON: A tragedy yes. Thank you. Yes. A tragedy.

KYLE: Hi, hey. Yeah yeah. I know. Well what can you do? I'll call you.

HAMILTON: Thank you. Yes. A shock to everyone. Yes. Thank you.

KYLE: Ah you wore the hat. She would have loved that. *(KYLE laughs.)* Oh stop it.

HAMILTON: A tragedy yes. Thank you.

KYLE: Hi hon. Oh I know. Such is life. You know? Exactly exactly.

HAMILTON: Thank you. It's all rather unreal to me still. Thank you.

KYLE: Hi there. Uh huh, uh huh. I know! We said no flowers in the paper, but they're from Andre. He's not so good at reading English. I know! Very tasteful considering Andre. I think they're from Ladybugs or Orchid In Bloom. Hamilton saw the card. *(to HAMILTON)* Are the flowers from Ladybugs or Orchid In Bloom?

HAMILTON: Pardon me?

KYLE: Are Andre's flowers from Ladybugs or Orchid In Bloom?

HAMILTON: They're from David Page Flowers.

KYLE: Really? *(to the mourner)* David Page, meh. Overpriced. Nice flowers but a bit of an *(mouths)* asshole. I showed him fourteen condos and he went with another agent. They ended up dating. Didn't last. Never does. I would have gone with Ladybugs. The guys at Ladybugs are hilarious. We'll get a drink later. Thanks. Oh listen I've got a new card. Here. *(fishes a card from his pocket)* Burn all former.

HAMILTON: Kyle, can I speak to you for a moment?

KYLE: Hm?

HAMILTON: Can I speak to you for a moment?

KYLE: Sure.

> *Quick light shift.*

HAMILTON: *(quiet and sharp)* What the hell are you doing?

KYLE: What?

HAMILTON: Handing out business cards?

KYLE: They're new. And it's not like the office ever closes in real estate. Everyone I meet is a potential client.

HAMILTON: Oh, so perhaps I should have brought along my portfolio?

KYLE: Maybe you should have, we're in the same business after all.

HAMILTON: No we're not! We most certainly are not! I design buildings, you sell buildings. Your buildings are already built!

KYLE: Hm, true. One can't build a building that's built. But me, I can sell them over and over and over again. It's like recycling. Real estate is very green. *(considering the angle)* There's something to that. I should make a note.

HAMILTON: This is a funeral!

KYLE: Well technically it's a visitation. The funeral is tomorrow.

HAMILTON: For our mother.

KYLE: Yes?

HAMILTON: Stop behaving like it's a cotillion.

KYLE: A cotillion?

HAMILTON: A cotillion.

KYLE: What's a cotillion?

HAMILTON: A cotillion a cotillion! A party where young ladies are presented to society!

KYLE: Oh, Mother would have liked that.

HAMILTON: Can you at least give the impression that you are sad?

KYLE: I am sad.

HAMILTON: You don't look sad. You don't sound sad.

KYLE: You don't sound sad either. You sound angry.

HAMILTON: I am angry! Our mother died tragically, horribly. At a parade!

KYLE: I think Mother would have liked that.

HAMILTON: Dying horribly?

KYLE: Dying at a parade.

HAMILTON: At a parade she attended at your behest.

KYLE: I didn't behest.

HAMILTON: You behested.

KYLE: I did not behest her.

HAMILTON: Perhaps not with words. Perhaps not consciously. Why else would Mother be at a Gay Days Parade if not for you?

KYLE: Why don't you just say it? It's my fault. I manslaughtered Mother!

They look out together suddenly.

HAMILTON & KYLE: *(to Father Glen)* Hello Father Glen.

KYLE: *(to Father Glen)* How would you feel about an aubergine vestment for the service? It's so regal.

HAMILTON: *(to KYLE)* Jesus Kyle!

HAMILTON & KYLE: *(to Father Glen)* Sorry Father Glen.

They listen.

HAMILTON: *(to Father Glen)* Oh yes Father Glen of course.

KYLE: The eulogy?

HAMILTON: *(to Father Glen)* Not a problem Father. I'll take that on. Of course of course. You can count on me certainly. As it should be.

KYLE looks at HAMILTON.

(to Father Glen) Thank you Father. I'll see you then.

Father Glen departs.

KYLE glares at HAMILTON.

What?

KYLE: Nothing.

HAMILTON: What?

KYLE: Nothing.

A moment.

"As it should be."

HAMILTON: What?

KYLE: Maybe I would have liked to take that on.

HAMILTON: You'd like to take that on?

KYLE: Maybe I might have.

HAMILTON: You'd like to do the eulogy?

KYLE: I might have maybe to have.

HAMILTON: You couldn't even write the obituary.

KYLE: I could've if you hadn't kept interrupting.

HAMILTON: Fine. Good. You do it.

KYLE: No no good. You do it.

HAMILTON: I was in Toastmasters.

KYLE: I could have been in Toastmasters.

HAMILTON: You took figure skating instead.

KYLE: They needed boys for dance pairs.

HAMILTON: You quit after a month.

KYLE: I have weak ankles.

HAMILTON: You want to do the eulogy do the eulogy.

KYLE: No you do it. "As it should be."

HAMILTON: Oh for God's sake!

    A moment.

Silence.

KYLE: No really. I'm fine with it.

HAMILTON: Good then.

KYLE: I am.

HAMILTON: Good.

Silence.

KYLE: I wouldn't mind just, you know, just, being there.

HAMILTON: Why wouldn't you be there?

KYLE: I mean there, with you. Up there with you. Quietly. Beside you. Up there. Quietly up there with you beside you.

HAMILTON: I guess that would be—

KYLE: Maybe introduce you.

HAMILTON: Introduce me?

KYLE: Or maybe that's not allowed. Not as it should be.

HAMILTON: I guess you could introduce me. Briefly.

KYLE: A brief introduction. That would be nice.

HAMILTON: Fine.

KYLE: Maybe say a word at the end.

HAMILTON: A word at the end?

KYLE: A word or two. At the end.

HAMILTON: Like what?

KYLE: Just something I'd plan. Something I'd write. Something I'd write and rehearse. Something I'd—

HAMILTON: Run by me?

KYLE: Something I'd run by you of course.

HAMILTON: Sure I guess that's fine.

KYLE: Thank you. You're a saint.

HAMILTON: There's no need for sarcasm.

KYLE: No I mean it really. A kind of a saint. For doing all you do. For taking Enzo. I would have taken him but my new building won't allow dogs. As I told you.

HAMILTON: Yes you told me.

KYLE: Pets of any kind.

HAMILTON: You mentioned.

KYLE: Dogs, birds, snakes. Any kind at all. Cats. A woman on the first floor snuck in a hamster. She was evicted.

HAMILTON: Yes you mentioned.

KYLE: Tragic.
     How's he doing, Enzo?

HAMILTON: He's getting a little agitated.

KYLE: That's to be expected.

HAMILTON: Yes.

KYLE: Will you do as I said, when he's alone in the house?

HAMILTON: He is in the kitchen, with a baby gate, yes, as you said.

KYLE: He's alone now?

HAMILTON: He is.

KYLE: For the first time?

HAMILTON: Yes.

KYLE: Jules isn't there.

HAMILTON: She is not.

KYLE: And she isn't here.

HAMILTON: No she is not.

KYLE: Where is she?

HAMILTON: At the club.

KYLE: Oh. Tennis?

HAMILTON: Curling.

KYLE: Good.

HAMILTON: "Good"?

KYLE: Good for Jules.

HAMILTON: I can't think why. She can drink when she's curling. It's like darts.

HAMILTON's cellphone rings. He looks at the call display.

Oh. That's Jules now. She's at home.

KYLE: Gosh, I hope nothing horrible happened.

HAMILTON: What?

KYLE: What?

HAMILTON: Why would something horrible have happened?

KYLE: Gosh I hope not.
I'll leave you to your call.

KYLE departs.

Slowly HAMILTON raises the phone to his ear.

HAMILTON: *(on phone, knowing something horrible has happened)* Hello...?

Light shift.

Music.

HAMILTON *produces the ladies' gloves from his pockets and puts them on, assuming the character of Bunny.*

HAMILTON AS BUNNY: After the summer of the sudden, strange night it was as suddenly winter.

Christmas Eve had been particularly two-dimensional that year. Hamilton's wife Jules was as usual absent, and her cranberry and spicy sausage stuffing felt as second-thought as her gift cards and her hardly-there apologies.

As a result Hamilton drank more than usual and very much "at" the situation with Jules. Now I don't judge a drink—or a dozen—but I have found that when one is drinking "at" something each drink creates a sloppier aim and anything can become a target. Kyle having watched *It's a Wonderful Life*—twice that evening—was characteristically cheery and oblivious to Hamilton's gunfire. Kyle's "date" however was feeling each and every shot. And to be honest I was shooting a bit from the hip myself—and mostly in the direction of Kyle's "escort," Gordon, a pleasant enough young man but with the distinct air of the pro about him. And when I say "pro" I'm not implying the professional world of bankers and doctors and let's just leave it at that.

Christmas done I decided my New Year's Eve would be spent in isolation. Just me and a shaker or two of the driest martinis, glued to my laptop, in pursuit of a virtual romance. Yet even warmly tipsy I couldn't muster the will to step into the web. Instead I stared blankly into my screen saver. Something called "arabesque." I had chosen it as my screen saver not because I knew it to be a ballet pose but because I had discovered after a brief investigation that "arabesque" was an artistic motif that constituted an infinite pattern of existence extending beyond the visible world. This was something I could drink not "at" but "with." And so I did, and I did, and I did. Some hours passed, then suddenly, in the green and blue strands of the DNA-like ever-infinite arabesque swirling before me in the deep dark empty nothingness of every possibility, I heard my own voice, from that strange July night: "I am going to get a dog."

Then I tumbled into a full evening of research. Midnight passed unnoticed because I had come upon the perfect breed. The Italian Greyhound. Two thousand years old. They had been around in Pompeii.

They didn't bark, they didn't shed, despite their alligator teeth they were gentle as lambs and they were loyal beyond description to their owners.

By three a.m. and about three hundred profiles in, suddenly chemistry. There was his face. There was Enzo. I melted at his eyes. His little paws. His perfect ears. His kind-of smile.

I called and woke the breeder on New Year's Day and made arrangements to have him flown in from Tennessee that very weekend. The moment I hung up the phone I knew everything was about to change.

Light shifts.

Music.

The Eulogy

A church.

KYLE stands awkwardly waiting, holding index cards.

HAMILTON enters, flustered.

They stand close, speaking quietly.

KYLE: You're late. Everyone's waiting.

HAMILTON: Don't speak to me.

KYLE: But I—

HAMILTON: Don't speak to me.

KYLE: But—

HAMILTON: Don't!

KYLE: I—

> *HAMILTON gestures to hit KYLE. KYLE flinches, the index cards go flying.*

> *Quickly KYLE gathers the index cards and approaches the podium, addressing the congregation.*

(reading from index cards) Good afternoon, ladies and gentlemen, friends and family. Thank you for joining us here today in our sadness. And loss. Our grief. And heartache. Our anguish, angst and pain. And woe. For those of you who do not know, but most of you do, I am Kyle Best and Bunny Best was my mother. But more than a mother. A friend. An inspiration. Beside me stands this handsome man.

HAMILTON looks askance at KYLE.

For those of you who do not know, but most of you do, this is Hamilton Best. My brother. And son as well to Bunny Best. Today Hamilton will offer in words a remembrance of Bunny.

Our mother. Our friend. Our family. Our matriarch. I look forward to hearing his remembrance today—told in the form of a eulogy—since Hamilton has always had with his words, a way. A path to the heart. With words. Thank you Hamilton.

HAMILTON moves to the podium but KYLE continues.

For agreeing to do this. Since we were boys Hamilton always knew the right word, the perfect phrase, the most excellent expression, idiom, axiom. Slogan… *(to HAMILTON)* I've lost my place.

HAMILTON: Thank you Kyle.

KYLE: Thank you.
Thank you.
Ladies and gentlemen, Hamilton Best. My brother.

KYLE steps away from the podium.

HAMILTON: Our mother was a woman who knew what she wanted. Once she tried everything.

> KYLE *chuckles.*

> HAMILTON *tries to ignore this.*

As Emma Goldman famously said, "If I can't dance to it, it's not my revolution." And that was my mother. From the time she was a young woman, her days working in the downtown core with immigrants and the underprivileged, she still found time to party nights away with the cream of the creative world and the city's intelligentsia. She would fight the best fight for something she believed in, but she always had a good time doing it.

> KYLE *chuckles.* HAMILTON *attempts to ignore him.*

As I was thinking about what I would say today, I was trying to distill our mother down to an anecdote, one day, that could sum up her spirit and her incredible love of living, that would speak to the place she held... she holds in all of our hearts. One anecdote, one day. But I couldn't find just one day.

> KYLE *steps to the podium, interrupting.*

KYLE: I could. Mother's Day. Every Mother's Day Hamilton would use all of his allowance to buy Mother something elaborate, something shiny and special and each Mother's Day I would make Mother a picture.

> HAMILTON *tries to push him gently away.*

HAMILTON: That's not one day Kyle.

KYLE: *(to HAMILTON)* Wait for it, wait for it.

> HAMILTON *steps away from the podium.*

(to the congregation) It wasn't really a picture I would make, it was more sculptural. Objects glued to cardboard. Collages. Mother loved the collages, simple and sad as they were. She loved Hamilton's elaborate, shiny gifts, but she made more of a show over the collages because of the effort I had put into them.
(to HAMILTON) And this is the one day.
(to the congregation) The one day. The Mother's Day when Hamilton came to me that Mother's Day morning and said, "Let's make something together."
(to HAMILTON) You remember this don't you?

HAMILTON: *(not sure where KYLE is going with this)* Yes I remember this.

KYLE: "Let's make something together." So we worked all morning on a portrait of Mother herself. But then a bottle of glue was knocked over and got into some solvent, which together created a toxic fume that gave me an allergic reaction, and Mother rushed us to the hospital and we ended up spending the whole day in emergency waiting to see a specialist to make sure I hadn't damaged my sinuses. And that Mother's Day in the hospital, as we were waiting, you went down to the cafeteria and you bought an Orange Crush. *(fighting back tears; to HAMILTON)* And you brought that Orange Crush upstairs. And we all shared it.
(to the congregation) That is the day. A mother. Her sons. A family, together. We shared the Orange Crush. We shared it.

HAMILTON: *(angry; to KYLE)* No we didn't. I gave the Orange Crush to Mother and then she gave it to you.

KYLE: Oh.

HAMILTON: You want one day? One day?

HAMILTON pushes KYLE away from the podium.

(to the congregation) Here's one day! The Thanksgiving with Candy and Dad where Mom gave us the wishbone. And it was supposed to be fair, but it wasn't! And we pulled the bone and I won the wish and Candy said good for me, and Dad said good for me, and drunk Uncle Desmond said good for me, but Mother said...
(to KYLE) You remember this? You remember this?!

KYLE: I think, yes.

HAMILTON: *(to KYLE)* Mother said: "Give your brother the wish. You don't need it!"

HAMILTON remembers they have an audience.

An extended uncomfortable moment.

KYLE: Thank you Hamilton.

HAMILTON, embarrassed, steps away from the podium. KYLE takes his place.

(to Uncle Desmond in the congregation) And you're looking great Uncle Desmond.
(to the congregation) So to finish, I would like to speak of someone who hasn't been mentioned at all today. Of someone who couldn't be here today. Someone who might very likely be suffering more than any of us. Maybe the most important someone in Mother's life.

HAMILTON: No no no no.

KYLE: The littlest Best.

HAMILTON: No no no.

KYLE: Of course I speak of Enzo.

HAMILTON: I could kill you.

KYLE: Mother's precious heart.

HAMILTON: I will.

KYLE: Our other brother.

HAMILTON: With my bare hands!

> HAMILTON *attempts to throttle* KYLE. *A tussle ensues.* HAMILTON *succeeds in throttling* KYLE.
>
> *Blackout.*

The Condolences (Part 1)

HAMILTON's house. The next day.

HAMILTON enters, crestfallen, a note in his hand.

KYLE enters with a box of sympathy cards.

HAMILTON discretely puts the note away.

KYLE sits; he reacts to a pain in his neck.

KYLE: Ow.

He rubs his neck and stretches it out.

Ahhh. Oooo.

HAMILTON: How's your neck?

KYLE: Better.
I understand now why you were so distracted at the funeral. I didn't know the dog had eaten your kitchen.

HAMILTON: My two-hundred-and-fifty-thousand-dollar kitchen.

KYLE: Mother always kept Enzo in the kitchen when he was distressed. It was easier to clean up the poo in the kitchen.

HAMILTON: Well he didn't poo.

KYLE: That's some consolation.

HAMILTON: He ate my Snaidero cupboards.

KYLE: Two-hundred-and-fifty-thousand dollars is a lot to pay for a kitchen.

HAMILTON: It wasn't my idea.

KYLE: How is Jules?

Silence.

She'll get over it.

Silence.

HAMILTON: Shall we do this?

KYLE: Fine.
So we'll need to respond to each.

HAMILTON: To each?

KYLE: To each condolence.

HAMILTON: Not individually.

KYLE: That's how it's done.

HAMILTON: It's not like a wedding. It's not like they brought gifts.

KYLE: They brought their grief.

HAMILTON: We can thank them all for that the same way.

KYLE: Some brought wishes, some brought prayers.

HAMILTON: We're not responding to everyone individually.

KYLE: It's required.

HAMILTON: Shall I check the etiquette?

KYLE: There should be some kind of difference between a response to say… Uncle Robert—this one is from Uncle Robert—and a response to say… her butcher.

HAMILTON: Her butcher?

KYLE: For example.

HAMILTON: Her *butcher*?

KYLE: For example.

HAMILTON: Oh. You mean like her milkman for example or her chimney sweep, or her lute instructor.

KYLE: Or her hairdresser for example.

HAMILTON: God, you live in a fantasy.

KYLE: Her hairdresser was there, and he brought a card.

HAMILTON: So he'll get the same thank you everyone else does.

KYLE: How about this. We respond en masse to each group. We could make groups. Each group would get their own tone. It would make less work.

HAMILTON: Fine.

KYLE: So. Let's make piles. Divide them into piles for each tone.

HAMILTON: Go ahead.

KYLE: How many piles should there be?

HAMILTON: I don't know.

KYLE: Two at least.

HAMILTON: Do you think?

KYLE: What should we call the first two piles?

HAMILTON: *(mocking)* Um… "Uncles" and "Hairdressers"?

KYLE: You mock me.

HAMILTON: You make it so easy.

KYLE: "Family" and "Friends."
Good.
Uncle Robert.
"Family."
There. *(dusts off his hands in a show of accomplishment)*

HAMILTON: You're enjoying this.

KYLE: I wouldn't say "enjoying."

HAMILTON: You're practically gleeful.

KYLE: Hardly.

HAMILTON: Dusting off your hands in a show of accomplishment?

KYLE: We're making progress.
    Monsieur Bisson.

HAMILTON: Monsieur Bisson?

KYLE: The gardener from the house.

HAMILTON: He came?

KYLE: And brought a card.

HAMILTON: Oh.

KYLE: "Friend"?

HAMILTON: One doesn't tip their "friends" at Christmas.

KYLE: Well he's not family.

HAMILTON: Well not friend.

KYLE: So…?

HAMILTON: Start another pile.

KYLE: Called?

HAMILTON: I don't know, "Other."

KYLE: That's not very specific.

HAMILTON: It's specific, it's other.

KYLE: Monsieur Bisson. "Other." There.

KYLE stars a third pile.

KYLE picks up a card.

Who's Patricia Tern?

HAMILTON: Is that the girl from the coffee place downtown?

KYLE: Which girl?

HAMILTON: The waitress from the place near the condo.

KYLE: No I think that's Mary-Lou or Ann-Marie or Heather or something.

HAMILTON: Put it in "Question."

KYLE: We don't have a pile called "Question."

HAMILTON: Well we goddamn well do now!

HAMILTON angrily takes the card and slams it down.

A moment.

KYLE: This is difficult, I know.

HAMILTON: It doesn't seem difficult for you.

KYLE: I'm in a different stage of grief.

HAMILTON: You don't seem to be grieving at all.

KYLE: Perhaps I had more time.

HAMILTON: How could you have had more time?

> *A beat.*

KYLE: Maybe I considered this kind of thing more.

HAMILTON: I doubt that. I doubt that you consider much at all other than when you last applied lip balm or mortgage rates or crickets in top hats.

KYLE: Hey! Lip balm is a lifesaver—for which I thank Mother—I can calculate a mortgage rate in my head in under a minute while discussing the view versus the square footage and Jiminy Crickets are sought-after collectables.

HAMILTON: *(incredulously)* Crickets in top hats.

KYLE: You're just resentful because Mother took me to see *Pinocchio* and she didn't take you.

HAMILTON: I had a riding lesson!
And I've since seen it; it's moralistic propaganda.

KYLE: Enough!
Crossed a line there.

A moment.

KYLE picks up a card.

(re: a card) Ew.

HAMILTON: What?

KYLE: Deirdre.

HAMILTON: Whore.

KYLE: Hamilton.

HAMILTON: She slept with Andre.

KYLE: So not "Friends"?

HAMILTON: Certainly not.

KYLE: "Other"?

HAMILTON: "No Response Required."

KYLE creates a fifth pile.

KYLE: *(happily)* "No Response Required!"

KYLE picks up the next card.

Oh.

HAMILTON: What?

KYLE: *(sweetly)* Aww.

HAMILTON: What?

KYLE: It's from Piña.

HAMILTON: Who?

KYLE: Piña from the float.

HAMILTON: The drunk drag queen who murdered our mother?!

KYLE: She wasn't drunk Hamilton.

HAMILTON: You don't call yourself Piña Colada and not have a drinking problem.

KYLE: You can't blame Piña.

HAMILTON: All right then. What about you Kyle? Mother never would have even been at a Gay Days Parade if not on the hunt for a husband for you.

KYLE: I don't need a husband.

HAMILTON: No you have Gordon. Gordon, that pinnacle of stability. Do you even know where he lives?!

KYLE: He moves a lot, but so do I.

HAMILTON: And why on earth would someone bring their sex worker home for Christmas dinner!

KYLE: He's not *my* sex worker, that's just what he does for a living!

HAMILTON: We both know very well how Mother felt about Gordon.

KYLE: You can't blame Gordon and you can't blame Piña and you can't blame me.

HAMILTON: Then who Kyle?

KYLE: Things just happen Hamilton.
Things just happen.

Silence.

(reading Piña's letter) "Dear Bestses."
Should be "Bests."
"The heavy nature of my heart knows no number of measure due to the terrible day of the weekend party of that terrible day. Words are hard to find and the silence will follow me to the end of the world. I will never sing again."
I don't think she technically sang.
"Love makes the world go round but at terrible times like at these love will feel more like a heartache. We must always remember the beauty that those lost have brought to our lives. How I will regret always her pretty little dog who made me lean down to give it a loving smile and which made my fall begin to end the life of such a mother as yours."

HAMILTON *slowly approaches the letter in* KYLE's *hand.*

I think that was very sweet.

HAMILTON *takes the letter from* KYLE.

HAMILTON: Her pretty little dog.

KYLE: I mean it's a bit clunky but her heart is in the right place.

HAMILTON: "Her pretty little dog who made me lean down."

KYLE: Oh.

> HAMILTON *tears the card in two and throws it into the box.*
> *He gathers the other cards into the box and thrusts the box*
> *at* KYLE.

HAMILTON: Go.

KYLE: Go?

HAMILTON: Take the cards and go.

KYLE: Maybe I should take Enzo.

HAMILTON: Go!

KYLE: Hamilton?

HAMILTON: NOW!

> *Light snaps out.*
>
> *Music.*
>
> HAMILTON *stands, some distance away is a dog cage.*
>
> *He holds the note from the top of the scene in his hand.*
>
> *After a moment.*

So here we are. The jig is, as it were, up. What do you have to say for yourself?

Oh, you're quiet now aren't you? Aren't you? And I know why. Oh I've always been on to you. I never fell for the "cute" thing. "Oh he's so adorable." Like Satan is adorable.

Oh don't give me that. Don't give me that tilted little head. Oh you're so innocent aren't you? "Huh? Who? Me?" Save it for your next victim. *(holds up the note)* You see this? You see this? You know what this is? It's a note from Jules. Left on the inedible Corian countertop of what remains of our two-hundred-and-fifty-thousand-dollar kitchen.

(reading the note to the dog) "Hamilton, this is the note we discussed years ago. The note we both promised we'd never write. It's become too much for me. For both of us. We live in separate rooms, separate worlds, separate compartments. And we have for years now.

You will probably think of this as an escape, if so imagine a burning building or a sinking ship. Know that I still care for you when I say, save yourself as well. Jules."

I'm sure it was entirely unnecessary to read the note. You probably wrote it for her. And then helped her pack. It was all part of your plan, wasn't it: kill his mother, destroy his home, get rid of his wife. What else do you have planned? Chew a few wires and guilelessly burn the whole place to the ground?

Don't look at me like that. "Oh what plan?" What plan indeed. Someone must be held accountable, it must be someone's fault. Nothing's random. Not anymore. Everything's planned now. Everything's prescribed. Pre-scribed. Scripted. Planned. Everything. From election outcomes to man-made weather systems to children's games.

Lego!

Even Lego has been corrupted.

It was my greatest joy as a boy. Running to the playroom and diving into my huge box of Lego. What shall it be today? A postmodern staircase? A cubist gazebo? A box with an opening in it? But now even Lego is prescribed.

First it was innocent. Some doors and windows, shutters, then the little people, then the wheels. Wheels! That was the real beginning of the end! The round things. Why were there suddenly round things? What could we do with the round bits? Then the hinges. We didn't used to need hinges before.

Then the plans! They don't sell Lego without a plan anymore. You can't just buy a box of Lego.

Now you have to buy the Norwegian airport or the ranch-style dream home or the Spanish town square! And I suppose there are the ingenious kids who might throw them all into a box together and after an afternoon come up with a Tower of Babel—but those minds are few and far between. Now we have hinges and wheels and round bits and little people! Now we have no need for imagination! Now there's a plan! What's the purpose of building a building that's already been planned?!

(suddenly hearing the question he's asking) What's the purpose of building a building that's already been planned?

Oh God.

Does nothing really matter?

Look at you. Dog. You really don't know, do you? You really have no idea. It's only this moment for you, isn't it? I envy you that. You gaze from your cage at a thing making noises. A thing that might feed you, or strike you, or throw you a ball. And if I were to feed you, you'd forget the moment hunger subsided, and if I were to strike you, you'd forgive at the sign of a treat, and if I were to throw you a ball... would you fetch it? For me?

Why don't you like me?

   Light shifts.

The Condolences (Part 2)

KYLE *enters wearing the gloves, having assumed the character of Bunny.*

KYLE AS BUNNY: On the way home from picking up Enzo at the airport he peed on me twice.

Within the first month he had chewed through two Marcel Breuer chairs and the base of my Noguchi coffee table and went through three trainers. The third trainer came along when at Doggie Day Care he had horrifyingly been labelled a "poo eater." By the second month I came to understand that breeders who said their dogs didn't bark were similar to parents who say their child doesn't cry. Both were liars.

Then there was the gift of the parasite. I shall never forget the mortification with which I called the owner of each and every dog he had been in contact with over the previous two weeks in order to share with them the diagnosis and the unfortunate news that they too might be forced into several rounds of antibiotics. I hadn't been so humbled since my twenties during a chlamydia scare in Amsterdam.

Then came the house-training. I was determined. I was determined to succeed. Those were dark days, days where I came to consider there might indeed be a vengeful force in the Universe, one that had sent this impossible challenge, this punishment, this cage of responsibility. I knew I had made the worst mistake of my life.

But then something happened. One afternoon in the dog park. He was some distance away humping—yes even without testicles this was a constant—but he was on the other side of the park humping a decrepit Dachshund while eyeing a miniature Poodle just out of her stitches.

To avoid the pinched wrath of the Poodle's mommy and the long-faced advice of the patronizing Dachshund's daddy, I called his name.

I called his name without hope, without desperation, having fully given up. And he stopped. He looked up. Over at me. And began running as if in slow motion and high speed all at the same time, toward me, across the vast expanse of park. He stopped before me. Placed his little rump down, tongue hanging out, almost a smile, and looked up at me. At me, the centre of his Universe. And then I fell in love.

Music.

Light shift.

KYLE's condo.

KYLE sits amid many small piles of cards on the floor. Also on the floor are the gloves he had been wearing as Bunny.

HAMILTON enters.

HAMILTON: Are those Mother's gloves?

KYLE: Oh. No. They're just something Gordon gave me. As a joke. For Halloween.

HAMILTON: To go as what?

KYLE: Just a lady.

HAMILTON: Last year I went as a piece of cheese.

KYLE: Was that funny?

HAMILTON: No.
We used to have imagination.

KYLE: Well a piece of cheese, that's an idea.

HAMILTON: I didn't have a choice. It was a cheese theme.

A moment.

How's Gordon?

KYLE: How do you mean?

HAMILTON: Just how is he?

KYLE: Oh. You hardly ever ask.

HAMILTON: Is he good?

KYLE: He's good. Busy.

HAMILTON bristles then recovers.

HAMILTON: *(offering some cards from his pocket)* You forgot a couple.

KYLE: Oh I've been having a hard time. Everything seems so independent of everything else. Uncle Robert, Aunt Fawn, Cousin Jean — that's easy. But Helene is more than just "Friend" since Deirdre went sour, and Maxine is more of an acquaintance since she got sober. And I can't really bring myself to "Other" too many, it seems so cold. And I don't have any more "Questions." People just don't seem to fit in piles if you know them. You know?

HAMILTON: Jules left.

KYLE: Left where?

HAMILTON: Left me.

KYLE: Oh.

HAMILTON: Just "oh"?

KYLE: Maybe it's for the best.

HAMILTON: Really?

KYLE: You don't like curling, do you?

HAMILTON: I hate it.

KYLE: I think she may have known that.

HAMILTON: You saw it coming?

KYLE: Since Christmas when she couldn't come to dinner. Who takes a Pilates class on Christmas day?

A moment.

HAMILTON: I noticed in your lobby downstairs just now two women with dogs.

KYLE: Oh.

HAMILTON: And a man with a cockatoo on his shoulder.

KYLE: Oh.

HAMILTON: They were all chatting with your concierge.

KYLE: Ah.

HAMILTON: All quite happily.

KYLE: I have a confession to make. Actually I have three.

HAMILTON: The first being?

KYLE: The building does take dogs.

HAMILTON: And birds apparently.

KYLE: And ferrets. A strange girl upstairs.

HAMILTON: And hamsters?

KYLE: But a woman on the first floor was evicted for feeding raccoons.

HAMILTON: I've heard they can be mean.

KYLE: I think Mother wanted you to have the dog. And so did I. And I didn't think he would eat your kitchen.

And this is my second confession. I did want him to poo on your floor. I thought you needed a little poo in your kitchen. Life is messy.

HAMILTON: Why?

KYLE: Why did I do that?

HAMILTON: Why is life messy?

KYLE: You always want everything ordered. In a line. On a grid. Under a heading. But everything doesn't always have a place. It just is.

HAMILTON: Everything doesn't necessarily fit in a pile.

KYLE: No.

HAMILTON: When we were little. Maybe eight and ten. Not long after Dad left. We were walking somewhere with Mother. You were beside her, I was behind. There was water. It was fall. You had on your peacoat and those brown lace-up boots.
Mother took off her hat and she had it in her hand. And with the other hand she was holding yours. But you kept pulling away. She would take your hand again and you would pull away. She was smiling, it was fine. She would take your hand, you would pull away. And I kept wishing it was my hand she was holding. I wished it was me. And I wouldn't pull away. I always wished it was me.

KYLE: She loved you best.

HAMILTON: But she loved you harder.

A moment.

What do I do now?

KYLE: Let her go?

HAMILTON picks up a card.

HAMILTON: What's this?

KYLE: Oh that's nothing, that's—

HAMILTON: "Enzo"?

KYLE: It's to Enzo.

HAMILTON opens the card.

HAMILTON: *(reading)* "Oh my poor little fellow, I can't imagine your sadness at this time. Know that when you cry you are not mourning who you lost but who you loved. Always remember your mommy loved you. Honeybee."
Who's Honeybee?

KYLE: That's his girlfriend.

HAMILTON gives him a look. KYLE shrugs.

They have a thing.

KYLE rises to leave.

HAMILTON: And what's your third confession?

KYLE considers this a moment, then:

KYLE: Mother was dying already. She told me. She saw the doctor. It was inoperable. All she didn't want was a long slow death with us around the bed changing her bedpans and checking her breathing. That's what she said. And that didn't happen.

KYLE reaches out to touch HAMILTON's shoulder.

HAMILTON pulls away. KYLE leaves.

Light fades.

Light up.

HAMILTON assumes the character of Bunny.

HAMILTON AS BUNNY: I don't know that I know what love is but I know that it makes dying harder. Dying is not necessarily that difficult; it's not like it's a surprise; it's not like we don't know it's coming eventually. Of course there are the odd curveballs. The runaway bus. The piano falling from a building. The sickly child. The fat Filipino man dressed as a female prostitute falling from a flatbed truck at a parade on a Sunday afternoon. There will always be the occasional oops.

But for those of us who've sat in the office across from the specialist and received the news, it really shouldn't be entirely out of the blue.

It's strange that according to the experts our first reaction is supposed to be shock. Mine wasn't.

I always knew that life was fatal; it wasn't a game I expected to win. And I always imagined I'd be all right with it. And I wasn't shocked, and there was no denial or bargaining or guilt or anger. And no depression.

But there was sadness. Because now I had… I won't say "fallen in love"… Learned to love? No. Let myself love. I'd let myself love. My children who'd grown bored by me, then embarrassed by me, then exasperated by me. The men who had left me. The friends who had betrayed me. The clerks and cab drivers. The flight attendants and receptionists. The call centre workers and canvassers. The tellers. The crossing guards. And Patricia, the girl at Pet Valu. All were precious to me.

What am I to do with this love?
What am I to do with all my love?

Light shifts.

The Will

Bunny's house.

KYLE *enters carrying a hat box and a couple of banker's boxes.*

HAMILTON *enters. He carries a document.*

HAMILTON: I found you.

KYLE: Oh. Yes. You found me.

HAMILTON: I went by your place. You weren't there.

KYLE: And you guessed I'd be here?

HAMILTON: No, I'm surprised actually. It's never been your favourite place, this house.

KYLE: So how did you—?

HAMILTON: Your concierge told me.

KYLE: Ah.

HAMILTON: You're chatty with your concierge.

KYLE: Yes. I'll have to work on that.

HAMILTON: It's odd seeing you all the time and then not seeing you for…

KYLE: A few days.

HAMILTON: A week.

KYLE: Have you been good?

HAMILTON: Have I been behaving?

KYLE: How are you feeling?

HAMILTON: Good.

KYLE: Really?

HAMILTON: No.
     Better.

KYLE: Better is good.

HAMILTON: Better is something.

KYLE: It must be a relief not having the dog.

HAMILTON: I'm sorry I just left him with your concierge.

KYLE: No that's fine.

HAMILTON: How is Enzo?

KYLE: He's sleeping.

HAMILTON: Really?

KYLE: We were at the park this morning.

HAMILTON: We never made it to the park.

KYLE: He likes the park.
I like the park.

HAMILTON: You always did.
I've been to the lawyer.

KYLE: *(re: document)* Is that it?

HAMILTON: Yes.
Do you want me to just tell you what it says?

KYLE: Why don't you read it.

HAMILTON: *(opens the document and reads it aloud)* I the undersigned
et cetera domiciled at et cetera in the city of so on make my last
will and testament as follows—

KYLE: Did she write that?

HAMILTON: It's standard.

KYLE: Why don't you just tell me what it says.

HAMILTON hands the document to KYLE.

HAMILTON: It's pretty much as we expected, fifty-fifty. The money the
stuff. The stuff I see you've started on.

KYLE: Yes.

HAMILTON: The condo, the land in France.

KYLE: She always wanted to build in France.

HAMILTON: I think we should hold on to the land.

KYLE: Yes. The condo will sell itself.

HAMILTON: And Mother wants you to have the house.

KYLE: Oh.

HAMILTON: I know you always thought of it as a tomb.

KYLE: A crypt. A mausoleum.

HAMILTON: But for what?

KYLE: A strand of Mother's DNA that I never got?
It always reminded me of who I was supposed to be but wasn't.

A moment.

HAMILTON: Maybe you should talk to Gordon about the house.

KYLE: Oh. Okay.

HAMILTON: Good. So, we're done then.

KYLE: Just one more thing.

KYLE retrieves a small sealed envelope from the hat box.

Mother wanted me to give you this.

HAMILTON: What is it?

KYLE: She wanted me to give it to you.

HAMILTON takes the envelope and opens it. A note. He reads it.

HAMILTON: Oh…

He folds it.

It just explains that she wants you to have Enzo.

KYLE: Really?

HAMILTON puts the note in his pocket.

HAMILTON: Yup.

KYLE: Because we did talk about it once and she said something different.

HAMILTON shrugs.

A moment.

HAMILTON: You know, Kyle…?
You are exactly who you should be.

KYLE: Thank you.

HAMILTON reaches out to shake KYLE's hand.

KYLE takes HAMILTON's hand and places it gently on his own heart.

HAMILTON gently cradles KYLE's cheek in the palm of his other hand.

HAMILTON *departs.*

Light.

Music.

Epilogue: A Dog Park

HAMILTON enters. He looks around the park. After a moment KYLE enters holding a leash.

HAMILTON: Hi.

KYLE: Hi.

HAMILTON: It's a big park.

KYLE: Did you have trouble finding it? We could have met at your place.

HAMILTON: No this is good.

KYLE: It's our second time here today.

HAMILTON: Where is he?

KYLE: Off somewhere. He always comes back.

HAMILTON: You were here already today?

KYLE: Mother was here with him three times a day.

HAMILTON: Is that why I hardly ever saw her anymore.

KYLE: No.

A moment.

HAMILTON: *(looking off)* There he is.

KYLE: *(looking off)* There he is.

HAMILTON: Oh my.

KYLE: What?

HAMILTON: What's he doing to that dog?

KYLE: That's Honeybee.

HAMILTON: They do have a thing.

> *HAMILTON looks over to another area of the park.*

He's popular.

KYLE: Who?

HAMILTON: The guy with the ponytail.

KYLE: Oh he thinks he's a dog whisperer. It's easy to be a dog whisperer with a pocket full of liver.

> *HAMILTON looks elsewhere with some interest. KYLE sees this.*

And that's Shy, but he's not shy at all.

HAMILTON: Oh, I thought that was a woman.

KYLE: Who?

HAMILTON: Shy.

KYLE: Shy's the dog. I don't know the owner's name. I don't know anybody's name. Or what they do for a living. Or their musical tastes, or their religious affiliation, or their political leaning, or their stand on the seal hunt or Israel.

KYLE waves at someone across the park.

(calling) Hey, how are you doing today? She got her cone off I see.

HAMILTON: Interesting.

KYLE: It's fantastic.

A moment.

HAMILTON takes Bunny's note from his pocket.

He considers it a moment then holds it out to KYLE.

What's that?

HAMILTON: Mother's note.

KYLE smiles, not taking the note.

KYLE: I know what it says.

A moment.

HAMILTON: Why did she tell you she was sick but she didn't tell me?

A moment.

KYLE: She knew it would be harder for you.

A moment.

HAMILTON considers the note. He puts it in his pocket.

He reaches out his hand to take the leash from KYLE.

Smiling, KYLE hands him the leash.

They step together toward where they see Enzo.

They stop and look at one another a moment.

Together they assume the character of Bunny.

KYLE AS BUNNY: To those who know the blood-stirring frosty dawns of September,

HAMILTON AS BUNNY: the explosive pride resulting from

KYLE & HAMILTON AS BUNNY: a command followed,

KYLE AS BUNNY: the traffic-stopping elation of

KYLE & HAMILTON AS BUNNY: a firm bowel movement, the healing power of

HAMILTON AS BUNNY: a wet nose on a tear-streaked cheek,

KYLE & HAMILTON AS BUNNY: the warm silence

KYLE AS BUNNY: of a sleeping dog,

HAMILTON AS BUNNY: to those I am talking about

KYLE & HAMILTON AS BUNNY: love.

KYLE AS BUNNY: It is as if this animal becomes

KYLE & HAMILTON AS BUNNY: our heart

KYLE AS BUNNY: and now we walk our hearts

KYLE & HAMILTON AS BUNNY: three times daily.

KYLE AS BUNNY: Some of us have hearts full of wonder and play…

HAMILTON AS BUNNY: …some of us have terrified hearts…

KYLE AS BUNNY: …some of us have hearts who won't listen and

KYLE & HAMILTON AS BUNNY: will go home with anyone.

HAMILTON AS BUNNY: When you can see someone's heart how bad can they be?

KYLE AS BUNNY: Hearts have no opinion.

HAMILTON AS BUNNY: No judgment.

KYLE AS BUNNY: So opinions have no meaning…

HAMILTON AS BUNNY: …judgments no purpose…

KYLE AS BUNNY: …when we walk with our hearts.

HAMILTON AS BUNNY: When we become that tiny.

KYLE AS BUNNY: And that large.

HAMILTON AS BUNNY: It's so simple.

They exit together.

Music.

End.